Look After Yourself

Your Hair

Look After Yourself

Your Hair

Claire Llewellyn

SEA-TO-SEA

Mankato Collingwood London

This edition first published in 2008 by
Sea-to-Sea Publications
1980 Lookout Drive
North Mankato
Minnesota 56003

Library of Congress Cataloging in Publication Data

Llewellyn, Claire.
    Your hair / by Claire Llewellyn.
        p.cm.
    ISBN 978-1-59771-097-8
    1. Hair--Juvenile literature. 2. Grooming for girls--Juvenile literature. 3. Grooming for boys--Juvenile literature. I. Title.

QM488.L54 2007
646.7'24--dc22

2006051280

9 8 7 6 5 4 3 2

Published by arrangement with the Watts Publishing Group Ltd, London.

Series editor: Sarah Peutrill
Art director: Jonathan Hair
Design: Kirstie Billingham
Illustrations: James Evans
Photographs: Ray Moller unless otherwise acknowledged
Picture research: Diana Morris
Series consultant: Lynn Huggins-Cooper

Acknowledgments:
Dr. Jeremy Burgess/Science Photo Library: 10cl
Eye of Science/Science Photo Library: 22b
Dr. Chris Hale/Science Photo Library: 24bl
Manfred Kage/Science Photo Library: 10bl
David Scharf/Science Photo Library: 8
Superstock: 21b
Andrew Syred/Science Photo Library: 24tr

With thanks to our models: Alice, Emilia, Holly, Jerome, Lewis, Mandalena, and Wilf

Contents

Looking at hair

There are many kinds of hair. Your hair may be curly or straight, thick or fine.

What's yours like?

Hair may be red, black, brown, fair, gray, or white.

Your hair helps to make you look like YOU!

A head of hair

A hair is a soft thread that grows out of the skin.

This picture shows two hairs much bigger than real life.

Most of us
have about
100,000 hairs
on our heads.

Heads get cold without hair.

About 50 hairs drop out every day. New hairs take their place.

Messy hair

Hair often gets messy, especially overnight.

My hair is a mess!

These hairs are magnified. This one is lying flat.

This hair is tangled.

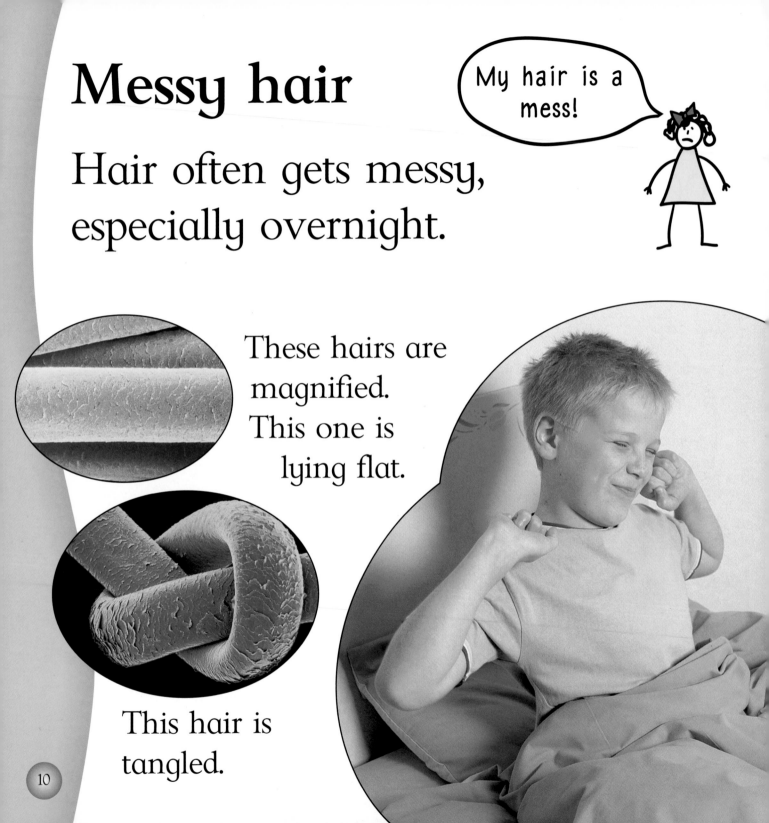

Brushing your hair
gets rid of tangles and
makes the hair
lie flat.

Always brush gently.

Brushes and combs

Keeping your hair tidy is easy.
All you need is a brush and comb.

Have I brushed my hair?

Brushes and combs soon get dirty. Wash them in soapy water.

Hair gets dirty

Each hair is coated with oil. Dirt sticks to the oil, making hair dirty.

Dirty hair looks bad.

When we are hot, our heads begin to sweat. Sweat makes our hair dirty, too.

Chlorine in swimming pools harms our hair.

Wash your hair after a swim.

Washing your hair

Wash your hair once
or twice a week.

My hair is
clean and
shiny.

1 Wet the hair.

2 Pour some
shampoo
onto your
hand.

3 Rub the shampoo into your hair.

4 Rinse off the bubbles with clean water.

5 Some people use conditioner on their hair. Follow the instructions on the bottle.

Drying your hair

Pat your wet hair with a towel. It is best to let hair dry on its own.

Try not to rub your hair or it will tangle.

If you do use a blowdryer, hold it away from your head.

Ouch! Blowdryers are hot!

19

Hairstyles

People wear their hair in all kinds of ways.

Look at my hair!

Our hairstyle is one of the things that makes us look different.

Having a haircut

As new hair grows from the root, the ends of the hair become weaker.

These hairs have been magnified.

In time they may split.

To keep it healthy
and strong, our hair
needs to be cut
every two months.

Hair grows
more quickly
in summer
than winter.

Before a haircut—and after.

Head lice

Tiny creatures called head lice like to live in hair.

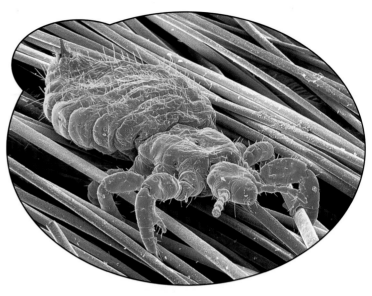

A magnified head louse

My head itches!

Their eggs (nits) look like tiny beads.

Head lice spread
easily from head
to head.

Most children get
head lice sometimes.

You need a
special shampoo
and comb to get
rid of head lice.

Healthy hair

Everyone wants healthy hair.

Look at my shiny hair!

Eating these foods will help make your hair grow strong.

Other foods help keep it healthy.

Drinking water is very good for your hair.

Remember to wash and brush your hair as well.

Glossary

chlorine   A strong-smelling gas used in swimming pools to keep the water clean.

conditioner A hair product that you put on your hair to make it soft and shiny.

fair   Having hair of a light color.

head lice (singular: **head louse**) Tiny insects that live in the hair.

magnified Made to look bigger.

nit   The egg of a head louse.

rinse   To wash away with water.

root	The part of the hair that grows under the skin.
shampoo	A liquid soap used for washing hair.
style	The way you choose to have your hair.
sweat	A salty, sticky liquid produced by the skin when you are hot. It helps to cool you down.
tangle	A small knot in the hair.
thread	A very thin strand of something.

Index

About this book

Learning the principles of how to keep healthy and clean is one of life's most important skills. **Look After Yourself** is a series aimed at young children who are just beginning to develop these skills. **Your Hair** looks at how to keep hair clean, tidy, and healthy.

Here are a number of activities children could try:

Pages 6-7 Collect photographs of people with different hair types.

Pages 8-9 Discuss how body hair helps to keep us warm—at cold temperatures hairs stand up, trapping warm air next to the skin. (As the hairs stand up we get goose pimples.)

Pages 10-11 Hold a section of hair near the root and run fingers carefully down the hair. Then do the same, but run the fingers up toward the root. With a little concentration, the hair feels smooth running down, but rough running up. This is because running fingers toward the root makes the scales stand up.

Pages 12-13 Ask children to design a comb or hairbrush that would be ideal for their own hair. Will the teeth or bristles be close or far apart, long or short? What kind of handle will it have?

Pages 14-15 Research the French pompadour—powdered styles—fashionable before the French Revolution. The hair was so dirty mice nested inside!

Pages 16-17 Collect a range of shampoos and conditioners and look at the instructions for using them. Are they all the same? Ask children to design their own shampoo labels. What will their shampoo do? What will it be called?

Pages 18-19 Write step-by-step instructions for using a blow dryer.

Pages 20-21 Conduct a survey of the different hairstyles in a class or group. Which is the most popular way to keep hair—short or long? Which is the favorite way for long hair to be worn?

Pages 22-23 Interview a hairdresser about his or her job.